A NOTE TO PARENTS

Reading Aloud with Your Child

Research shows that reading books aloud is the single most valuable support parents can provide in helping children learn to read.

- Be a ham! The more enthusiasm you display, the more your child will enjoy the book.
- Run your finger underneath the words as you read to signal that the print carries the story.
- Leave time for examining the illustrations more closely; encourage your child to find things in the pictures.
- Invite your youngster to join in whenever there's a repeated phrase in the text.
- Link up events in the book with similar events in your child's life.
- If your child asks a question, stop and answer it. The book can be a means to learning more about your child's thoughts.

Listening to Your Child Read Aloud

The support of your attention and praise is absolutely crucial to your child's continuing efforts to learn to read.

- If your child is learning to read and asks for a word, give it immediately so that the meaning of the story is not interrupted. DO NOT ask your child to sound out the word.
- On the other hand, if your child initiates the act of sounding out, don't intervene.
- If your child is reading along and makes what is called a miscue, listen for the sense of the miscue. If the word "road" is substituted for the word "street," for instance, no meaning is lost. Don't stop the reading for a correction.
- If the miscue makes no sense (for example, "horse" for "house"), ask your child to reread the sentence because you're not sure you understand what's just been read.
- Above all else, enjoy your child's growing command of print and make sure you give lots of praise. *You are your child's first teacher — and the most important one. Praise from you is critical for further risk-taking and learning.*

— Priscilla Lynch
Ph.D., New York University
Educational Consultant

Thanks to Dr. Petra Sierwald,
The Field Museum of Natural History,
Chicago, IL

For Emily
— F.R.

For Emily
— J.D.Z.

Text copyright © 1996 by Fay Robinson.
Illustrations copyright © 1996 by Jean Day Zallinger.
All rights reserved. Published by Scholastic Inc.
HELLO READER!, CARTWHEEL BOOKS, and the CARTWHEEL BOOKS
logo are registered trademarks of Scholastic Inc.

Library of Congress Cataloging-in-Publication Data

    Robinson, Fay.
  Mighty spiders! / by Fay Robinson ; illustrated by Jean Day Zallinger.
        p.   cm. — (Hello reader! Level 2)
          ISBN 0-590-26262-9
      1. Spiders — Juvenile literature. [1. Spiders.]   I. Zallinger, Jean,
ill.   II. Title.   III. Series.
QL452.2.R635   1996   95-10530
595.4'4 — dc20   CIP
                                                 AC

12 11 10 9 8 7 6 5 4 3 2 1   6 7 8 9/9 0 1/0

Printed in the U.S.A.   09

First Scholastic printing, May 1996

Mighty Spiders!

by Fay Robinson
Illustrated by Jean Day Zallinger

Hello Science Reader ! — Level 2

SCHOLASTIC INC.
Cartwheel
·B·O·O·K·S·®

New York Toronto London Auckland Sydney

Spiders up.

Spiders down.

Mighty spiders all around!

Eight strong legs.
Tough, hard skin.

Silky webs to scurry in.

Spiders anywhere you please —

on the ground

and high in trees.

Under water,

sand,

and stone.

Spiders creeping in your home.

Green and yellow.

Flashy pink.

White like snowflakes.

Black like ink.

Spider stripes

and starry thorns.

Spider hearts

and spider horns.

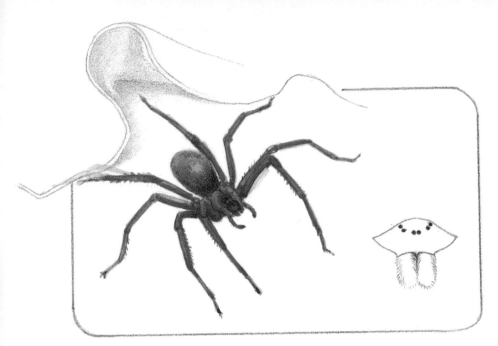

Six eyes,

eight eyes,
large and small.

Spiders with no eyes at all.

Spiders small as grains of sand.

Spiders bigger than your hand.

Spiders spin a silky thread —
a thread that sometimes
makes a web.

Webs in tangles.

Webs in wheels.

Webs for catching
spider meals —

a moth, a wasp,
a juicy fly.

Any bug that wanders by.

Other spiders stalk and hunt,
doing mighty spider stunts.

Spiders hiding,

spiders creeping,

spiders diving,

spiders leaping.

Snatching insects,

birds, or frogs,

lizards, fish,
or pollywogs.

Mothers make a silk cocoon.
Tiny eggs inside hatch soon.

Babies crawling from their sac.

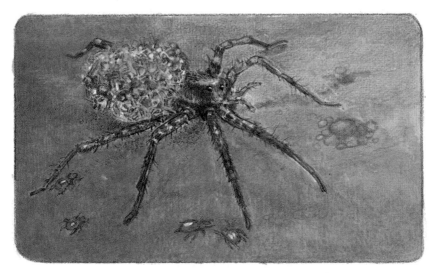

Babies riding piggyback.

Babies shedding too-small skin.

Babies blowing in the wind.

Spiders up and spiders down.
Mighty spiders all around!

Cover:
Black Widow

Page 4:
American House
Spider

Page 5:
American House
Spider

Page 6:
Black and Yellow
Garden Spider

Page 7:
Burrowing Wolf Spider

Page 7:
Pink-toed Tarantula

Page 8:
European Water Spider

Page 8:
Dancing White Lady

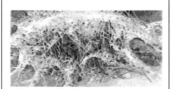

Page 9:
Mediterranean Tent
Builder

Page 9:
American House Spider

Page 10:
Green Huntsman Spider

Page 10:
Heather Spider

Page 11:
White Crab Spider

Page 11:
Black Widow

Page 12:
Zebra Spider

Page 14:
Wolf Spider

Page 19:
Marbled Spider

Page 12:
Spiny-backed Spider

Page 15:
Cave Spider

Page 20:
Barn Spider

Page 13:
Bolas Spider

Page 16:
Dwarf Spider

Page 21:
Trapdoor Spider

Page 13:
Spiny-backed Spider

Page 17:
Red-legged Tarantula

Page 22:
Green Lynx Spider

Page 14:
Brown Recluse Spider

Page 18:
Bowl and Doily Spider

Page 22:
European Water Spider

31

Page 23:
Jumping Spider

Page 24:
Jumping Spider

Page 24:
Bird-eating Spider

Page 25:
Fishing Spider

Page 26:
Nursery Web Spider

Page 26:
Black Widow Spider
with spiderlings

Page 27:
Wolf Spider with
spiderlings

Page 27:
Orb Weaver

Page 28:
Nursery Web
Spiderlings

Page 29:
Monkey Spiderlings